County Catalogue of Unusual Commonwealth War Graves and Memorials

Vol. 1 – Shropshire

by

Martin P Nicholson

CONTENTS

INTRODUCTION

This book is compiled from the records maintained by the Commonwealth War Graves Commission of servicemen and women killed or missing since the start of the First World War in 1914.

The first list contains details of the location of the grave or memorial in Shropshire naming servicemen or women who were one of five or less of their particular service rank who lost their lives.

The second list contains details of the location of the grave or memorial in Shropshire naming servicemen or women who were one of five or less of their particular regiment or service who lost their lives.

Every life lost as a result of military service is a tragedy for the family and friends of the individual, and this book does not seek to imply that those listed here are any more deserving of memory than those not selected. The book shows the wide range of units from which only a handful, or even a single, life was lost, and also the wide range of ranks where also only a handful, or even a single, holder of that rank is commemorated in Shropshire.

The CWGC lists 307,131 names of dead and missing service personnel and members of the Merchant Navy who are remembered at locations in the United Kingdom. Of these just over 1,000 (0.3%) are to be found in Shropshire.

In a small number of cases the official CWGC stone does not appear in the listed location. We have seen examples where it has been replaced by a stone designed by the family and on a few occasions a lengthy search for a missing stone has been unsuccessful.

Rank - Unique

There are 31 service personnel with war graves or their names on memorials in Shropshire who are the only representatives with their particular service rank.

1, Air Mechanic, Royal Air Force, DUCKERS, FREDRICK HENRY, MARKET DRAYTON CEMETERY, P. 52.

2, Air Mechanic 3rd Class, Royal Air Force, FREEMAN, MUNSLOW (ST. MICHAEL) CHURCHYARD EXTENSION, In North part.

3, Aircraftwoman 1st Class, Women's Auxiliary Air Force, BACCHUS, HEATHER, DONINGTON (ST. CUTHBERT) CHURCHYARD, ALBRIGHTON , Row 12. Grave 15.

4, Aircraftwoman 2nd Class, Women's Auxiliary Air Force, TODD, MARGARET GWENDOLINE, WOMBRIDGE (SS. MARY AND LEONARD) CHURCHYARD, Grave 719.

5, Assistant Waitress, Queen Mary's Army Auxiliary Corps, PICKERING, MALINSLEE (ST. LEONARD) CHURCHYARD, In North-West part.

6, Boy 2nd Class, Royal Navy, PRICE, SHREWSBURY GENERAL CEMETERY, 12. I. D. **(Photo)**

7, Brigadier General, Devonshire Regiment, JACSON, MAINWARING GEORGE, HAUGHTON (ST. CHAD) CHURCHYARD, East 1. 1.

8, Chief Stoker, Royal Navy, GREEN, SYDNEY, HENGOED (ST. BARNABAS) CHURCHYARD, N.E. of church.

9, Colour Serjeant, King's Shropshire Light Infantry, LEAH, SHREWSBURY GENERAL CEMETERY, 61. 13. **(Photo)**

10, Cook, Royal Navy, LLOYD, GILBERT, CORELEY (ST. PETER) CHURCHYARD, North of church.

11, Corporal Wheeler, Royal Army Service Corps, FERRINGTON, ROWTON (ALL HALLOWS) CHURCHYARD, East of Church, in old ground.

12, Craftsman, Royal Electrical and Mechanical Engineers, O'REILLY, THOMAS PATRICK, SHREWSBURY GENERAL CEMETERY, Extn. Plot 10. Grave 416. **(Photo)**

13, Engine Room Artificer 5th Class, Royal Navy, BATES, CHARLES WILLIAM CECIL, SHREWSBURY GENERAL CEMETERY, 192. 15. B. **(Photo)**

14, Group Captain, Royal Air Force, SHERRIFF, FREDERICK GEORGE, DONINGTON (ST. CUTHBERT) CHURCHYARD, ALBRIGHTON , Row 13. Grave 9.

15, Leading Seaman, Royal Navy, HILL, LUDLOW OLD CEMETERY, In South part.

16, Lieut-Commander, Royal Naval Volunteer Reserve, ROGERS-COLTMAN, JULIAN COLTMAN, WENTNOR (ST. MICHAEL) CHURCHYARD EXTENSION, Row A. Grave 16.

17, Lieut-Commander (A), Royal Naval Volunteer Reserve, WATSON, JAMES CHRISTIAN VICTOR KIERO, HINSTOCK CHURCH BURIAL GROUND, Row 27. Grave 1.

18, Lieutenant (A), Royal Naval Volunteer Reserve, RIDLEY, RICHARD HERBERT, BRIDGNORTH CEMETERY, Grave 1064.

19, Lieutenant Colonel, Shropshire Yeomanry, TAYLEUR, LITTLE DRAYTON (CHRIST CHURCH) CHURCHYARD, In North part.

20, Naval Airman 2nd Class, Royal Navy, SIMPSON, EDWARD HORACE, HINSTOCK CHURCH BURIAL GROUND, Row 27. Grave 2.

21, Ordinary Signalman, Royal Navy, CALVERT, WILLIAM ANDREW, ONIBURY (ST. MICHAEL) CHURCHYARD, East of church.

22, Ordinary Telegraphist, Royal Navy, PRYCE, WILFRED HENRY, SHREWSBURY GENERAL CEMETERY, Extn. Plot 9. Grave 161.

23, Petty Officer Stoker, Royal Navy, CLARKE, THOMAS WALTER, CLEOBURY MORTIMER CEMETERY, Grave 245.

24, Quartermaster Serjeant, South Lancashire Regiment, DAVIES, WHITCHURCH CEMETERY, 156

25, Recruit, King's Shropshire Light Infantry, GRIFFIN, SHREWSBURY GENERAL CEMETERY, 83. 3. C. **(Photo)**

26, Regimental Serjeant Major, South Lancashire Regiment, SCRIVEN, PREES (ST. CHAD) CHURCHYARD, On North boundary.

27, Sister, Queen Alexandra's Imperial Military Nursing Service, TONGE, MARY ISABEL, SHREWSBURY GENERAL CEMETERY, Extn. Plot 10. Grave 302.

28, Staff Serjeant Major, Army Service Corps, KEENAN, TILSTOCK (CHRIST CHURCH) CHURCHYARD EXTENSION, 39

29, Stoker 1st Class, Royal Navy, DEEGAN, RAYMOND DORRIEN COLLINGWOOD, SHREWSBURY GENERAL CEMETERY, Extn. Plot 9. Grave 442.

30, Volunteer, Auxiliary Territorial Service, BARNICUT, CONSTANCE, SHREWSBURY GENERAL CEMETERY, Extn. Plot 10. Grave 425. **(Photo)**

31, Worker, Queen Mary's Army Auxiliary Corps, JONES, WELSHAMPTON (ST. MICHAEL) CHURCHYARD, In South West part, on West boundary.

13628 COL. SERJT.
J. LEAH
KING'S SHROPSHIRE L.I.
11TH MAY 1915

14527959 CRAFTSMAN
T. P. O'REILLY
R.E.M.E.
22ND JANUARY 1945   AGE 31

Rank - Two examples known

There are 22 service personnel with war graves or their names on memorials in Shropshire who share their rank with only one other representative with their particular service rank.

32, Air Mechanic 1st Class, Royal Air Force, CLACK, TILSTOCK (CHRIST CHURCH) CHURCHYARD EXTENSION, 38

33, Air Mechanic 1st Class, Royal Air Force, DYKE, TREFONEN CEMETERY, D. 3. 64.

34, Cadet, Royal Flying Corps, BROWN, SHAWBURY (ST. MARY THE VIRGIN) CHURCHYARD, South East part.

35, Cadet, Royal Navy, GATLIFF, JOHN CAULFEILD WOLSELEY, ALVELEY (ST. MARY) CHURCHYARD, Near North boundary

36, Company Serjeant Major, Royal Defence Corps, LANGLEY, WELLINGTON GENERAL CEMETERY, SHROPSHIRE , 3. 1769.

37, Company Serjeant Major, King's Shropshire Light Infantry, TAYLOR, WILLIAM JOHN, BASCHURCH (ALL SAINTS) CHURCHYARD, F. 12.

38, Ordinary Seaman, Royal Naval Volunteer Reserve, BARLOW, WILLIAM, LUDLOW (HENLEY ROAD) CEMETERY, B. 5. 736.

39, Ordinary Seaman, Royal Navy, LONGSTAFF, JOHN THOMAS, DONNINGTON WOOD (ST. MATTHEW) CHURCHYARD, New Ground. Row 14. Grave 6.

40, Petty Officer, Royal Navy, ANDREWS, HAROLD, SHREWSBURY GENERAL CEMETERY, Extn. Plot 10. Grave 516. **(Photo)**

41, Petty Officer, Royal Navy, KENNETT, SHREWSBURY GENERAL CEMETERY, 192. 13. G.

42, Squadron Leader, Royal Air Force Volunteer Reserve, DAVIES, PHILIP FRANCIS, BRIDGNORTH CEMETERY, Grave 1791.

43, Squadron Leader, Royal Air Force, SPEER, LIONEL EDWARD, SHAWBURY (ST. MARY THE VIRGIN) CHURCHYARD, Row 18. Grave 6.

44, Squadron Quartermaster Serjeant, King's Shropshire Light Infantry, ALLEN, FREDERICK WILLIAM, SHREWSBURY GENERAL CEMETERY, 199. 5. A. **(Photo)**

45, Squadron Quartermaster Serjeant, Army Service Corps, HEALEY, MARKET DRAYTON CEMETERY, AF. Gen. 63.

46, Staff Nurse, Queen Alexandra's Imperial Military Nursing Service, HUGHES, GLADYS CORFIELD, NANTMAWR CONGREGATIONAL CHAPELYARD, 3.6.

47, Staff Nurse, Queen Alexandra's Imperial Military Nursing Service, TEGGIN, EUGENIE ELIZABETH, ST. MARTIN'S CHURCHYARD, SHROPSHIRE , In old ground North East of Church.

48, Sub-Lieutenant (A), Royal Naval Volunteer Reserve, BUCHAN, WALTER GAIR, CHILDS ERCALL (ST. MICHAEL) CHURCHYARD, East portion.

49, Sub-Lieutenant (A), Royal Naval Volunteer Reserve, DAVIES, FRANCIS HENRY, CLUN CEMETERY, Sec. N. Row 26. Grave 224.

50, Warrant Officer Class I, Royal Tank Regiment, R.A.C. , DENTON, WALTER CYRIL, ST. GEORGE'S (ST. GEORGE) CHURCHYARD, OAKENGATES , Extn. N.E. part.

51, Warrant Officer Class I, King's Shropshire Light Infantry, FARMER, ALBERT STANLEY, SHREWSBURY GENERAL CEMETERY, Extn. Plot 10. Grave 505. **(Photo)**

52, Wing Commander, Royal Air Force, FINNY, ARTHUR WILLIAM MAGEE, STOKE-UPON-TERN (ST. PETER) CHURCH CEMETERY, Row H. Grave 252.

53, Wing Commander, Royal Air Force, TOLAND, GERALD THOMAS, MORETON CORBET (ST. BARTHOLOMEW) CHURCHYARD, South of church.

H. ANDREWS
PETTY OFF. R.N. P/SSX. 17971
H.M.S. "VERNON"
8TH MARCH 1944 AGE 25

4026380 W.O.I (RSM)
A. S. FARMER
THE KING'S
SHROPSHIRE LIGHT INFANTRY
29TH JANUARY 1940 AGE 38

Rank - Three examples known

There are 21 service personnel with war graves or their names on memorials in Shropshire who share their rank with only two other representatives with their particular service rank.

54, Able Seaman, Royal Navy, BROWN, RAYMOND G., SHREWSBURY GENERAL CEMETERY, Extn. Plot 1 Grave 107. **(Photo)**

55, Able Seaman, Royal Navy, DODINGTON, ALICK GILROY, HOPE (HOLY TRINITY) CHURCHYARD, WORTHEN , South of church.

56, Able Seaman, Royal Naval Volunteer Reserve, JARVIS, WELLINGTON GENERAL CEMETERY, SHROPSHIRE , I. 2044.

57, Company Quartermaster Serjeant, King's Shropshire Light Infantry, EWERS, TOM HERBERT, SHREWSBURY GENERAL CEMETERY, 197. I. B. **(Photo)**

58, Company Quartermaster Serjeant, King's Shropshire Light Infantry, JONES, FREDERICK ARTHUR, WENLOCK (BROSELEY) CEMETERY, N.C. 1034.

59, Company Quartermaster Serjeant, King's Shropshire Light Infantry, WELCH, ARTHUR REGINALD, SHREWSBURY GENERAL CEMETERY, Extn. Plot 5. Grave 262.

60, Lance Bombardier, Royal Artillery, ASHLEY, ALFRED ERIC, BARROW (ST. GILES) CHURCH CEMETERY, N.E. part.

61, Lance Bombardier, Royal Garrison Artillery, DAVIES, JOSEPH HAROLD, OSWESTRY GENERAL CEMETERY, H. N.C. 221.

62, Lance Bombardier, Royal Artillery, JONES, RAYMOND, WROCKWARDINE WOOD (HOLY TRINITY) CHURCHYARD, S.W. of church.

63, Leading Stoker, Royal Navy, EATON, LOPPINGTON (ST. MICHAEL) CHURCHYARD, South of Church, boundary of new ground.

64, Leading Stoker, Royal Navy, JONES, WELLINGTON GENERAL CEMETERY, SHROPSHIRE , 4. 3113.

65, Leading Stoker, Royal Navy, MARTIN, ERNEST TAFT, HIGHLEY (ST. MARY) CHURCHYARD, East part of churchyard.

66, Private 2nd Class, Royal Air Force, DAVIES, THOMAS GEORGE, WORTHEN (ALL SAINTS) CHURCHYARD

67, Private 2nd Class, Royal Air Force, JONES, THOMAS JOHN, SHREWSBURY GENERAL CEMETERY, 197. 9. F. **(Photo)**

68, Private 2nd Class, Royal Air Force, OGDEN, STOKE-UPON-TERN (ST. PETER) CHURCH CEMETERY, I. 4. 132.

69, Staff Serjeant, The Glider Pilot Regiment, A.A.C. , DYER, JOHN CHARLES, WHITCHURCH CEMETERY, Grave 781.

70, Staff Serjeant, Royal Engineers, ELLIS, DAVID WILLIAM, HENGOED (ST. BARNABAS) CHURCHYARD, North of church.

71, Staff Serjeant, Army Service Corps, MOORE, MUCH WENLOCK CEMETERY, 58

72, Trooper, Royal Armoured Corps, MASON, KENNETH FREDERICK, QUATFORD (ST. MARY MAGDALENE) CHURCHYARD, N.W. of church.

73, Trooper, Reconnaissance Corps, R.A.C. , MORRIS, ROBERT, BISHOP'S CASTLE (ST. JOHN THE BAPTIST) CHURCHYARD, S.E. of church.

74, Trooper, Reconnaissance Corps, R.A.C. , SHOTTER, CHARLES ALBERT, SHREWSBURY GENERAL CEMETERY, Extn. Plot 10. Grave 417. **(Photo)**

7576 C. QMR. SERJT.
T. H. EWERS
KING'S SHROPSHIRE L.I.
18TH OCTOBER 1918 AGE 28

Rank - Four examples known

There are 4 service personnel with war graves or their names on memorials in Shropshire who share their rank with only three other representatives with their particular service rank.

75, Pioneer, Royal Engineers, DAWES, SHREWSBURY GENERAL CEMETERY, 192. 3. H. **(Photo)**

76, Pioneer, Royal Engineers, PARKER, SHREWSBURY GENERAL CEMETERY, 145. 13. F.

77, Pioneer, Royal Engineers, ROGERS, GEORGE WILLIAM, SHREWSBURY GENERAL CEMETERY, 2. 13. A.

78, Pioneer, Royal Engineers, WICKS, JAMES HAROLD, WELLINGTON GENERAL CEMETERY, SHROPSHIRE , 2. 2735.

Rank - Five examples known

There are 15 service personnel with war graves or their names on memorials in Shropshire who share their rank with only four other representatives with their particular service rank.

79, Flight Lieutenant, Royal Air Force Volunteer Reserve, CLARK, JOHN HOPE, HOPE BOWDLER (ST. ANDREW) CHURCHYARD, South of church.

80, Flight Lieutenant, Royal Air Force Volunteer Reserve, HUGHES, DOUGLAS, MARKET DRAYTON CEMETERY, Sec. E. Grave 57.

81, Flight Lieutenant, Royal Air Force Volunteer Reserve, JOHNSON, GEORGE EARL, CULMINGTON (ALL SAINTS) CHURCHYARD, South of chancel.

82, Flight Lieutenant, Royal Air Force Volunteer Reserve, PHILLIPS, ROY HAROLD, DONINGTON (ST. CUTHBERT) CHURCHYARD, ALBRIGHTON , Row 13. Grave 11.

83, Flight Lieutenant, Royal Air Force, PINCHES, MAURICE HENRY, BOURTON CHURCHYARD, N.E. of church.

84, Fusilier, Royal Welch Fusiliers, CAINE, HAROLD, BRIDGNORTH CEMETERY, Grave 579A.

85, Fusilier, Lancashire Fusiliers, FRANCE, ARTHUR, LITTLE DRAYTON (CHRIST CHURCH) CHURCHYARD, S.E. part of church.

86, Fusilier, Royal Welch Fusiliers, GADSDEN, WILLIAM RICHARD, SHREWSBURY GENERAL CEMETERY, Extn. Plot 10. Grave 424. **(Photo)**

87, Fusilier, Royal Welch Fusiliers, GLOVER, GEORGE ARTHUR, SHREWSBURY GENERAL CEMETERY, Extn. Plot 10. Grave 423.

88, Fusilier, Royal Welch Fusiliers, MORRIS, SAMUEL, OSWESTRY GENERAL CEMETERY, Sec. X. Grave 292.

89, Marine, Royal Marines, CLAY, WILLIAM COLIN, WHITCHURCH CEMETERY, Grave 871.

90, Marine, Royal Marines, DAVIES, PETER ALFRED, SHREWSBURY GENERAL CEMETERY, Extn. Plot 8. Grave 250.

91, Marine, Royal Marines, EDWARDS, WILLIAM STANLEY, WESTON RHYN (ST. JOHN) CHURCHYARD, S.W. part of churchyard.

92, Marine, Royal Marines, LLOYD, WILLIAM EDWARD, WENLOCK (BROSELEY) CEMETERY, Cons. Grave 1407.

93, Marine, Royal Marines, OWEN, ALFRED RICHARD, CONDOVER (SS. MARY AND ANDREW) CHURCH CEMETERY, Row 1 Grave 1.

Unique military unit

There are 46 service personnel with war graves or their names on memorials in Shropshire who are the only representatives of their particular military unit.

1, 4th Dragoon Guards (Royal Irish), Private, BOYLING, ELLESMERE CEMETERY, SHROPSHIRE, A. 92.

2, 16th (The Queen's) Lancers, Private, BROWN, WHITTON (ST. MARY) CHURCHYARD, 195

3, 20th Hussars, Private, JARMAN, BRIDGNORTH CEMETERY, 307

4, African Pioneer Corps (East Africa), Private, NGANDA KADUGALA, SHREWSBURY GENERAL CEMETERY, Extn. Plot 10. Grave 518. **(Photo)**

5, Argyll and Sutherland Highlanders, Lieutenant, SUTTHERY, DORIAN MELBOURNE, MARKET DRAYTON CEMETERY, E. 179.

6, Army Veterinary Corps, Private, SHERWOOD, CHARLES, SHREWSBURY GENERAL CEMETERY, Spec. Memorial. (Plot 10, Grave 300A).

7, Border Regiment, Private, WILSON, WHITCHURCH CEMETERY, 1100

8, Cameronians (Scottish Rifles), Rifleman, MARSHALL, DONALD, PONTESBURY (ST. GEORGE) CHURCH CEMETERY, South part.

9, Cheshire Yeomanry, Serjeant, PLATT, TREFONEN CEMETERY, B. 2. 72.

10, Corps of Military Police, Lance Corporal, SOMERS, JAMES FREDERICK, SHREWSBURY GENERAL CEMETERY, Extn. Plot 5. Grave 361.

11, Dorsetshire Regiment, Private, PURSLOW, ERNEST JAMES, ASTERLEY CHURCHYARD, S.E. of church.

12, Durham Light Infantry, Captain, HUGHES-GAMES, SHREWSBURY GENERAL CEMETERY, 161. 8. G.

13, East Lancashire Regiment, Private, SCOTT, CHARLES EDWARD, NEWPORT CEMETERY, SHROPSHIRE, 987

14, East Surrey Regiment, Private, TODD, THOMAS, OSWESTRY GENERAL CEMETERY, Sec. T. Grave 254.

15, General List, Major, PLOWDEN, HUMPHREY ROGER HENRY, PLOWDEN (ST. WALBURGA) ROMAN CATHOLIC CHURCHYARD, South part of churchyard.

16, Gordon Highlanders, Private, CAIN, JOHN, SHREWSBURY GENERAL CEMETERY, Extn. Plot 10. Grave 508.

17, Hampshire Regiment, Private, MILLINGTON, WILLIAM HENRY, SHREWSBURY GENERAL CEMETERY, Extn. Plot 10. Grave 418.

18, Highland Light Infantry (City of Glasgow Regiment), Serjeant, BRAIDWOOD, GEORGE WALKER, SHREWSBURY GENERAL CEMETERY, Extn. Plot 10. Grave 296. **(Photo)**

19, Imperial Camel Corps, Private, OLIVER, WESTON RHYN (ST. JOHN) CHURCHYARD, 237

20, King's Own Yorkshire Light Infantry, Captain, YATES, FRANCIS WILLIAM, DONINGTON (ST. CUTHBERT) CHURCHYARD, ALBRIGHTON, South of West end of Church.

21, London Regiment, Private, JONES, JOHN ROWLAND, OSWESTRY GENERAL CEMETERY, F. N.C. 155.

22, London Regiment (London Scottish), Private, McMICHAEL, COLIN JOHN WYLD, BRIDGNORTH CEMETERY, 523 J.

23, London Regiment (Post Office Rifles), Rifleman, CONNOLLY, WALTER PERCY, SHREWSBURY GENERAL CEMETERY, 200. 10. A.

24, Machine Gun Corps, Major, DOUGLAS, SHREWSBURY GENERAL CEMETERY, 200. I. C.

25, Machine Gun Corps (Heavy Branch), Lance Corporal, HARPER, COUND (ST. PETER) CHURCHYARD, 385

26, Middlesex Regiment, Corporal, TURNER, ROBERT, QUATFORD (ST. MARY MAGDALENE) CHURCHYARD, N.E. of church.

27, Northamptonshire Regiment, Private, LOUGHMON, GEORGE ABBOTT, TILSTOCK (CHRIST CHURCH) CHURCHYARD EXTENSION, 73

28, Northamptonshire Yeomanry, Major, CUNLIFFE, JOHN BROOKE, PETTON CHURCHYARD, Near main door of Church.

29, Queen's Own (Royal West Kent Regiment), Corporal, EDWARDS, WILLIAM FRANCIS, MUCH WENLOCK CEMETERY, 739

30, Queen's Own Royal West Kent Regiment, Private, SHEEHAN, PATRICK JOSEPH, SHREWSBURY GENERAL CEMETERY, Extn. Plot 10. Grave 415.

31, Royal Armoured Corps, Trooper, MASON, KENNETH FREDERICK, QUATFORD (ST. MARY MAGDALENE) CHURCHYARD, N.W. of church.

32, Royal Army Pay Corps, Second Lieutenant, WOODS, WILLIAM JOHN, OSWESTRY GENERAL CEMETERY, Sec. Z. Grave 53.

33, Royal Dublin Fusiliers, Lance Corporal, BUTTERWORTH, HENRY, BRIDGNORTH CEMETERY, 336

34, Royal Fusiliers (City of London Regiment), Corporal, WENLOCK, FRANK, WROCKWARDINE (ST. PETER) CHURCH CEMETERY, Grave C.176.

35, Royal Inniskilling Fusiliers, Captain, SAUNDERS, OSWESTRY GENERAL CEMETERY, T. N.C. 240.

36, Royal Munster Fusiliers, Private, PUGH, SHREWSBURY GENERAL CEMETERY, 191. 9. C.

37, Royal Pioneer Corps, Private, PARMEE, GEORGE HENRY, SHREWSBURY GENERAL CEMETERY, Extn. Plot 12. Grave 258. **(Photo)**

38, Royal Scots, Private, DUTTON, JAMES ALFRED, OSWESTRY GENERAL CEMETERY, U. C.E. 387.

39, Royal Scots Fusiliers, Private, SAUNDERS, SHREWSBURY GENERAL CEMETERY, II. 14. H.

40, Royal Sussex Regiment, Private, CLARKE, BOURTON CHURCHYARD, West of Church.

41, Royal Tank Regiment, R.A.C., Warrant Officer Class I, DENTON, WALTER CYRIL, ST. GEORGE'S (ST. GEORGE) CHURCHYARD, OAKENGATES, Extn. N.E. part.

42, Royal Ulster Rifles, Rifleman, HAMAR, EVAN JOHN EDWARD, NEWCASTLE (ST. JOHN THE EVANGELIST) CHURCHYARD

43, The Glider Pilot Regiment, A.A.C., Staff Serjeant, DYER, JOHN CHARLES, WHITCHURCH CEMETERY, Grave 781.

44, Welch Regiment, Serjeant, BUNTIN, WILLIAM ERNEST, WENLOCK (CASTLE GREEN) CEMETERY, Grave C.10.

45, Welsh Horse Yeomanry, Private, WYCHERLEY, JAMES EDWIN, LOPPINGTON (ST. MICHAEL) CHURCHYARD, South West of Church.

46, Yorkshire Hussars Yeomanry, Private, PREECE, FREDERICK, LUDLOW (HENLEY ROAD) CEMETERY, B. 9. 820.

Unit - Two examples known

There are 30 service personnel with war graves or their names on memorials in Shropshire who are 1 of only 2 representatives of their particular military unit.

47, Army Ordnance Corps, Lance Corporal, MORRIS, CLEOBURY MORTIMER CEMETERY, 811

48, Army Ordnance Corps, Private, RUTH, WHITCHURCH CEMETERY, 1305

49, Black Watch (Royal Highlanders), Lieutenant, FOSTER-BARHAM, THOMAS, STOKE-UPON-TERN (ST. PETER) CHURCH CEMETERY, Row G. Grave 244.

50, Black Watch (Royal Highlanders), Private, STEVENS, CHARLES THOMAS, WROCKWARDINE WOOD (HOLY TRINITY) CHURCHYARD, South of church.

51, Devonshire Regiment, Private, DAVIS, MADELEY (ST. MICHAEL) CHURCHYARD, In North-East Extn.

52, Devonshire Regiment, Brigadier General, JACSON, MAINWARING GEORGE, HAUGHTON (ST. CHAD) CHURCHYARD, East 1. 1.

53, East Yorkshire Regiment, Private, GOUGH, RICHARD EDWARD, CHURCH STRETTON (CUNNERY ROAD) CEMETERY, M. 25.

54, East Yorkshire Regiment, Private, PICKERSGILL, SHREWSBURY GENERAL CEMETERY, 178. 2. A.

55, Military Police Corps, Serjeant, PIM, TILSTOCK (CHRIST CHURCH) CHURCHYARD EXTENSION, 20

56, Military Police Corps, Lance Corporal, WEBB, NEWPORT CEMETERY, SHROPSHIRE, 2284

57, Montgomeryshire Yeomanry, Private, MORGAN, RICHARD JOHN, LLANYMYNECH (ST. AGATHA) CHURCHYARD, In new ground.

58, Montgomeryshire Yeomanry, Private, WIGLEY, ALBERT, CARDESTON (ST. MICHAEL) CHURCHYARD, In South West part.

59, Northumberland Fusiliers, Private, MURRAY, ANDREW, SHREWSBURY GENERAL CEMETERY, 51. 16. A. **(Photo)**

60, Northumberland Fusiliers, Private, SMITH, SHREWSBURY GENERAL CEMETERY, 198. 6. H.

61, Queen Mary's Army Auxiliary Corps, Worker, JONES, WELSHAMPTON (ST. MICHAEL) CHURCHYARD, In South West part, on West boundary.

62, Queen Mary's Army Auxiliary Corps, Assistant Waitress, PICKERING, MALINSLEE (ST. LEONARD) CHURCHYARD, In North-West part.

63, Reconnaissance Corps, R.A.C., Trooper, MORRIS, ROBERT, BISHOP'S CASTLE (ST. JOHN THE BAPTIST) CHURCHYARD, S.E. of church.

64, Reconnaissance Corps, R.A.C., Trooper, SHOTTER, CHARLES ALBERT, SHREWSBURY GENERAL CEMETERY, Extn. Plot 10. Grave 417. **(Photo page 15)**

65, Royal Army Veterinary Corps, Private, BEESTON, WILLIAM GEORGE, CHESWARDINE (ST. SWITHUN) CHURCHYARD, Near North gate.

66, Royal Army Veterinary Corps, Captain, HARDING, GEORGE CLIFFORD, CHURCH STRETTON (CUNNERY ROAD) CEMETERY, K. 6.

67, Royal Electrical and Mechanical Engineers, Serjeant, LEWIS, JOHN STANLEY, ALBRIGHTON (ST. MARY MAGDALENE) CHURCHYARD, New Ground. Row B. Grave 21.

68, Royal Electrical and Mechanical Engineers, Craftsman, O'REILLY, THOMAS PATRICK, SHREWSBURY GENERAL CEMETERY, Extn. Plot 10. Grave 416.

69, Royal Fusiliers, Corporal, GRIFFITHS, WESTON LULLINGFIELDS (HOLY TRINITY) CHURCHYARD, North-West of Church.

70, Royal Fusiliers, Private, ONSLOW, ALBERT FLETCHER, SHREWSBURY GENERAL CEMETERY, 157. S. H. **(Photo)**

71, Royal Marine Artillery, Private, POOLER, KEMBERTON (ST. ANDREW) CHURCHYARD, South-East of Church.

72, Royal Marine Artillery, Corporal, ROSSITER, ERNEST WILLIAM, HADLEY GENERAL CEMETERY, 712

73, Royal Marine Light Infantry, Private, ELLIOTT, SHIFNAL (ST. ANDREW) CHURCHYARD, Screen Wall. (12. 2.)

74, Royal Marine Light Infantry, Private, JONES, JOHN ALFRED, OSWESTRY GENERAL CEMETERY, E. C.E. 245.

75, Royal Naval Reserve, Lieutenant, DAVIES, OSWESTRY GENERAL CEMETERY, D. C.E. 58/59.

76, Royal Naval Reserve, Lieutenant, LIDDELL, ASHFORD BOWDLER (ST. ANDREW) CHURCHYARD, In new ground.

Unit - Three examples known

There are 21 service personnel with war graves or their names on memorials in Shropshire who are 1 of only 3 representatives of their particular military unit.

77, Army Pay Corps, Corporal, BROOKS, SHREWSBURY GENERAL CEMETERY, 51. 2. H. **(Photo)**

78, Army Pay Corps, Corporal, FOWLES, WEM (SS. PETER AND PAUL) CHURCH CEMETERY, 21. 28.

79, Army Pay Corps, Corporal, TILLETT, LUDLOW OLD CEMETERY, South-West of Church.

80, Bedfordshire Regiment, Private, DABBS, JOHN HERBERT, WELLINGTON GENERAL CEMETERY, SHROPSHIRE, 2. 1424.

81, Bedfordshire Regiment, Private, EVANS, PULLOXHILL (ST. JAMES) CHURCHYARD, Under the War Memorial.

82, Bedfordshire Regiment, Captain, GARNETT-BOTFIELD, CHARLES SIDNEY, MORTON (SS. PHILIP AND JAMES) CHURCHYARD, New ground. 9. 20.

83, Monmouthshire Regiment, Private, DAVIES, CHARLES WILLIAM, WHITCHURCH CEMETERY, 152

84, Monmouthshire Regiment, Private, FORTUNE, PONTESBURY (ST. GEORGE) CHURCH CEMETERY, B. 90.

85, Monmouthshire Regiment, Private, WHITTINGHAM, MARKET DRAYTON CEMETERY, E. 182.

86, Oxford and Bucks Light Infantry, Private, HARRIS, BASCHURCH (ALL SAINTS) CHURCHYARD, F. 7.

87, Oxford and Bucks Light Infantry, Private, HIGGS, BRIDGNORTH CEMETERY, 345

88, Oxford and Bucks Light Infantry, Serjeant, KIRK, LOUIS EDWARD, NEWPORT CEMETERY, SHROPSHIRE, 1701

89, Queen Alexandra's Imperial Military Nursing Service, Staff Nurse, HUGHES, GLADYS CORFIELD, NANTMAWR CONGREGATIONAL CHAPELYARD, 3.6.

90, Queen Alexandra's Imperial Military Nursing Service, Staff Nurse, TEGGIN, EUGENIE ELIZABETH, ST. MARTIN'S CHURCHYARD, SHROPSHIRE, In old ground North East of Church.

91, Queen Alexandra's Imperial Military Nursing Service, Sister, TONGE, MARY ISABEL, SHREWSBURY GENERAL CEMETERY, Extn. Plot 10. Grave 302.

92, Shropshire Yeomanry, Private, EDWARDS, WHITCHURCH CEMETERY, 1169

93, Shropshire Yeomanry, Private, LEA, ELLESMERE CEMETERY, SHROPSHIRE, G. 106.

94, Shropshire Yeomanry, Lieutenant Colonel, TAYLEUR, LITTLE DRAYTON (CHRIST CHURCH) CHURCHYARD, In North part.

95, The Loyal North Lancashire Regiment, Private, COLLINSON, OSWESTRY GENERAL CEMETERY, T. N.C. 215.

96, The Loyal North Lancashire Regiment, Private, JONES, TILSTOCK (CHRIST CHURCH) CHURCHYARD EXTENSION, 52

97, The Loyal North Lancashire Regiment, Private, MORRIS, GEORGE THOMAS, WEM (SS. PETER AND PAUL) CHURCH CEMETERY, 23. 18.

Unit - Four examples known

There are 32 service personnel with war graves or their names on memorials in Shropshire who are 1 of only 4 representatives of their particular military unit.

98, Auxiliary Territorial Service, Volunteer, BARNICUT, CONSTANCE, SHREWSBURY GENERAL CEMETERY, Extn. Plot 10. Grave 425. **(Photo page 8)**

99, Auxiliary Territorial Service, Lance Corporal, LUNN, ELSIE HELENA MARY, HOPESAY (ST. MARY) NEW CHURCHYARD, N.W. part.

100, Auxiliary Territorial Service, Private, TROWELL, NOREEN, SHREWSBURY GENERAL CEMETERY, Extn. Plot 10. Grave 515.

101, Auxiliary Territorial Service, Corporal, WHEELER, MARY AGNES, CLUN (ST. GEORGE) CHURCHYARD, South of church.

102, Home Guard, Private, BROWN, ARTHUR DENNIS, HADLEY GENERAL CEMETERY, Yellow. Grave 1520.

103, Home Guard, Lieutenant, HOPWOOD, FRANK CYRIL, CLUN (ST. GEORGE) CHURCHYARD, South of church.

104, Home Guard, Lieutenant, MASSEY, REGINALD EUSTACE, BITTERLEY (ST. MARY) CHURCHYARD, South of church near porch.

105, Home Guard, Private, PEARSON, FRANK, ALBRIGHTON (ST. MARY MAGDALENE) CHURCHYARD, New Ground. Row 1. Grave 19.

106, King's Royal Rifle Corps, Lance Corporal, BOMFORD, HENRY RAYMOND, BADGER CHURCH CEMETERY, In North-East part.

107, King's Royal Rifle Corps, Rifleman, GRIFFITHS, SHREWSBURY GENERAL CEMETERY, Spec.Memorial (Plot 10, Grave 299A)

108, King's Royal Rifle Corps, Rifleman, PUGH, GEORGE, SHREWSBURY GENERAL CEMETERY, 27. 16. C.

109, King's Royal Rifle Corps, Rifleman, TIMMS, SHREWSBURY GENERAL CEMETERY, 197. 8. H.

110, Labour Corps, Private, CAKEBREAD, HENRY ALFRED, OAKENGATES (HOLY TRINITY) CHURCHYARD

111, Labour Corps, Private, HARVEY, NEWPORT CEMETERY, SHROPSHIRE, 1708

112, Labour Corps, Private, MOSS, TILSTOCK (CHRIST CHURCH) CHURCHYARD EXTENSION, 36

113, Labour Corps, Private, WILSON, OSWESTRY GENERAL CEMETERY, T. N.C. 248.

114, North Staffordshire Regiment, Warrant Officer Class II, HILL, ALFRED JAMES, SHREWSBURY GENERAL CEMETERY, Extn. Plot 10. Grave 300.

115, North Staffordshire Regiment, Private, TWEEN, JOSEPH, ALBRIGHTON (ST. JOHN THE BAPTIST) CHURCHYARD

116, North Staffordshire Regiment, Private, WESTON, WILLIAM, WOORE (ST. LEONARD) CHURCHYARD, In North-West corner.

117, North Staffordshire Regiment, Private, WILLIAMS, ALFRED, OSWESTRY GENERAL CEMETERY, F. 333.

118, South Staffordshire Regiment, Private, CORNS, HARRY, ALBRIGHTON (ST. MARY MAGDALENE) CHURCHYARD, 18. 12.

119, South Staffordshire Regiment, Private, DAVIES, WORFIELD (ST. PETER) CHURCHYARD, South West of church.

120, South Staffordshire Regiment, Private, MATTHEWS, SHREWSBURY GENERAL CEMETERY, 197. 9. A.

121, South Staffordshire Regiment, Corporal, WILLIAMS, WILLIAM JOHN SAMUEL, WORFIELD CHURCH CEMETERY, N.W. part.

122, Women's Auxiliary Air Force, Aircraftwoman 1st Class, BACCHUS, HEATHER, DONINGTON (ST. CUTHBERT) CHURCHYARD, ALBRIGHTON, Row 12. Grave 15.

123, Women's Auxiliary Air Force, Corporal, CUNLIFFE, FRANCES ANN, DONINGTON (ST. CUTHBERT) CHURCHYARD, ALBRIGHTON, Row 12. Grave 10.

124, Women's Auxiliary Air Force, Corporal, METCALFE, KATHLEEN VIVIENNE, DONINGTON (ST. CUTHBERT) CHURCHYARD, ALBRIGHTON, Row 12. Grave 16.

125, Women's Auxiliary Air Force, Aircraftwoman 2nd Class, TODD, MARGARET GWENDOLINE, WOMBRIDGE (SS. MARY AND LEONARD) CHURCHYARD, Grave 719.

126, Worcestershire Regiment, Serjeant, COOPER, BRIDGNORTH CEMETERY, 811

127, Worcestershire Regiment, Private, CORFIELD, DODDINGTON (ST. JOHN THE BAPTIST) CHURCHYARD, SHROPSHIRE, In South East part.

128, Worcestershire Regiment, Private, GWILT, ABDON (ST. MARGARET) CHURCHYARD, Near South-West boundary.

129, Worcestershire Regiment, Private, TROW, KINLET (ST. JOHN THE BAPTIST) CHURCHYARD, North of Church.

Unit - Five examples known

There are 25 service personnel with war graves or their names on memorials in Shropshire who are 1 of only 5 representatives of their particular military unit.

130, King's Own (Royal Lancaster Regiment), Private, DAVIES, WILLIAM, OSWESTRY GENERAL CEMETERY, T. N.C. 219.

131, King's Own (Royal Lancaster Regiment), Lance Corporal, HAMPSON, OSWESTRY GENERAL CEMETERY, T. N.C. 246.

132, King's Own (Royal Lancaster Regiment), Private, MANSELL, YOCKLETON (HOLY TRINITY) CHURCHYARD, West of Church.

133, King's Own (Royal Lancaster Regiment), Private, SHOTTON, STANTON-UPON-HINE HEATH (ST. ANDREW) CHURCHYARD, On North boundary.

134, King's Own (Royal Lancaster Regiment), Private, THOMAS, KNOWBURY (ST. PAUL) CHURCHYARD, South West of Church.

135, Manchester Regiment, Lance Corporal, ASHLEY, WEM (SS. PETER AND PAUL) CHURCH CEMETERY, 21. 25.

136, Manchester Regiment, Private, BICKLEY, LEONARD WALLACE, WELLINGTON GENERAL CEMETERY, SHROPSHIRE, Grave 0409.

137, Manchester Regiment, Private, FOX, LITTLE WENLOCK (ST. LAWRENCE) CHURCHYARD, In North-East corner.

138, Manchester Regiment, Private, MATHESON, WHITCHURCH CEMETERY, 142

139, Manchester Regiment, Private, SABIN, WORTHEN (ALL SAINTS) CHURCHYARD

140, Rifle Brigade, Rifleman, BAILEY, FRANK EDWARD, SHREWSBURY GENERAL CEMETERY, 199. 7. F. **(Photo)**

141, Rifle Brigade, Rifleman, BRIGHT, SHREWSBURY GENERAL CEMETERY, 205. 15. G.

142, Rifle Brigade, Rifleman, EDWARDS, HIGH ERCALL (ST. MICHAEL) CHURCHYARD, NI. I. 5.

143, Rifle Brigade, Major, HAMILTON-RUSSELL, ARTHUR GUSTAVUS LINDSEY, BURWARTON (ST. LAWRENCE) OLD CHURCHYARD, North part of churchyard.

144, Rifle Brigade, Lieutenant, MOSTYN-OWEN, DAVID LITTLETON, HAUGHTON (ST. CHAD) CHURCHYARD, East of church.

145, Royal Marines, Marine, CLAY, WILLIAM COLIN, WHITCHURCH CEMETERY, Grave 871.

146, Royal Marines, Marine, DAVIES, PETER ALFRED, SHREWSBURY GENERAL CEMETERY, Extn. Plot 8. Grave 250.

147, Royal Marines, Marine, EDWARDS, WILLIAM STANLEY, WESTON RHYN (ST. JOHN) CHURCHYARD, S.W. part of churchyard.

148, Royal Marines, Marine, LLOYD, WILLIAM EDWARD, WENLOCK (BROSELEY) CEMETERY, Cons. Grave 1407.

149, Royal Marines, Marine, OWEN, ALFRED RICHARD, CONDOVER (SS. MARY AND ANDREW) CHURCH CEMETERY, Row 1 Grave 1.

150, Welsh Regiment, Private, BONNER, ASTLEY (ST. MARY) CHURCHYARD, SHROPSHIRE, South of main path.

151, Welsh Regiment, Lance Corporal, JONES, JOHN CECIL, WEM (SS. PETER AND PAUL) CHURCH CEMETERY, 5. 231.

152, Welsh Regiment, Private, LAWTON, SAMBROOK (ST. LUKE) CHURCHYARD, 451

153, Welsh Regiment, Corporal, RICHARDS, GEORGE HENRY, ALVELEY (ST. MARY) CHURCHYARD, Near North boundary.

154, Welsh Regiment, Private, WEAVER, DODDINGTON (ST. JOHN THE BAPTIST) CHURCHYARD, SHROPSHIRE, North West of Church.

By the same author and available from Amazon

The Grave Hunters Series

Gravestones of Shropshire

Unusual Gravestones

Gravestones of Herefordshire (due late 2015)

County Catalogue of Unusual War Graves and Memorials

Volume 1 – Shropshire

Volume 2 – Worcestershire

Volume 3 – Herefordshire

Volume 4 – Staffordshire (due autumn 2015)

Unusual Commonwealth War Graves and Memorials

Volume 1 – United Kingdom

Volume 2 – Belgium (due autumn 2015)

Volume 3 – France (due autumn 2015)

The Western Front Series

The Arras War Graves and Memorials

The Menin Gate Memorial

Thiepval War Graves and Memorials

Tyne Cot War Graves and Memorials